MW01251758

HERE'S HOW
TO BE HEALTHY

BY

BENGAMIN GAYELORD
HAUSER

TEMPO BOOKS, INC.
580 FIFTH AVENUE
NEW YORK CITY, N. Y.

Printing Statement:

Due to the very old age and scarcity of this book, many of the pages may be hard to read due to the blurring of the original text, possible missing pages, missing text and other issues beyond our control.

Because this is such an important and rare work, we believe it is best to reproduce this book regardless of its original condition.

Thank you for your understanding.

HERE'S HOW TO BE HEALTHY

By Bengamin Gayelord Hauser

COCKTAILS! What visions of tall, tinkling, appetite-stirring glasses the mere thought of them brings to our minds—and our palates! Martini, Dubonnet, Alexander, Manhattan—man's mind has certainly been fertile in inventing new thrills to arouse jaded appetites and stimulate failing spirits.

But now—Health Cocktails!

No, they are not made of gin or whiskey with a single pickled cherry or olive floating disconsolately in its acrid bath. Here are zesty, tangy juices of fresh young vegetables and ripe fruit; green and yellow, sweet and tart, they sparkle in the cocktail glasses and are a revelation to those of us who have had to be satisfied day after day with the juice of the orange, the grapefruit, the tomato. There are adventure and taste thrills in this newly discovered health realm—yes, and health abundant. Come with me; I'll be your guide along the Trail of the Cocktail Shaker.

Back in 1914 a dramatic experiment was carried on in America which for a few short but vivid weeks occupied the spotlight in the news. Twelve convicts, six of them murderers, were promised unconditional pardons if they would volunteer for a test that would prove to science whether or not, and to what extent, a mineral-deficient diet affects health.

The results were startling. The twelve convicts, the "Poison Squad," as the newspapers called them, were so affected by the mineral-deficient diet that although they knew pardon awaited them at the end of the sixty-day period, they refused after only a few days to go on with the experiment. Several of them tried to commit suicide. Two showed symptoms of pellagra, and six others actually developed the disease. There was a great hubbub of excitement. Letters, telegrams of protest, petitions were sent to the prison officials.

And then, as a final step in the experiment, the prisoners were put on a mineral-complete ration, and were soon restored to health.

This experiment showed that without doubt deficiency of any one of the sixteen important mineral elements causes sickness in some form. The problem of the diet specialist is to find those foods that contain the necessary minerals in the proper proportion. These foods of high mineral content are sure to be rich in the mysterious vitamins, which are essential to health. And the mineral-rich diet abounding in vitamins is sure to give increased pep and vitality.

The search of the scientists for foods with these qualifications is not difficult. Dozens of fruits and vegetables from Nature's bountiful storehouse contain these organic minerals and vitamins. Their alkaline reaction in the body offsets the acid by-products of starch and protein digestion and prevents acidosis.

WHYS AND WHEREFORES

"But why vegetable cocktails," you ask, "when you can get the same benefits from fresh vegetables and fruits?"

But can you?

Here are some of the answers to that question which will convince you of the value of the vitamin-rich, mineral-rich juices contained in Health Cocktails:

To begin with, you get the raw juice of fruits and vegetables, full of living energy. No matter how scientifically it is carried on, cooking causes chemical changes that always destroy some of this energy.

Here is a little experiment that will show you just how true this statement is. Put some pineapple juice, squeezed out of a raw, fresh pineapple, in a glass. Into it drop a bit of hard-boiled egg white, which is almost one hundred per cent protein. Now watch it. What happens? You will see that some of the egg will actually disappear in the solution in a day or two—it has been digested! But put some of the hard-boiled egg white into pineapple juice that has been heated. It will take days and days for the same thing to happen.

This is because raw pineapple juice contains a marvelous enzyme, a digestive agent, which helps to digest protein foods like nuts, meat and egg white. But once the pineapple juice is heated, the enzyme is made less active, and the digestive powers of the juice are greatly lessened.

And, too, the vitamins which abound in raw fruit and vegetable juices of all sorts are at least partly destroyed by cooking.

That is one reason. Here is another: Health Cocktails, because of their concentrated goodness, are the quickest means of revitalizing the body.

It is quite true that you can rechemicalize and revitalize the body with whole fresh fruits and vegetables. But you cannot do so as quickly as you can with the juices. In fact it would be almost impossible to eat enough fruit or vegetables to get the minerals and chemicals found in a quart of juices. The bulk and roughage would be too filling, too cumbersome for our digestive and eliminative systems to handle.

This principle has been recognized in many countries. In France a one-day "juice regimen" has been successfully used under the name of "La Cure des Fruits." For one day each week the diet is restricted to fruit and vegetable juices. In that day enough organic alkaline elements are absorbed by the system to counteract the effects of the occasional indiscretions to which we are prone—too much to eat at a banquet or too rich refreshments at the Wednesday afternoon bridge. In Germany the one-day dietetic holiday, the "Gesundheitstag," has thousands of followers.

The popularity of this diet in all countries where it has been tried is undoubtedly largely due to the fact that it is a diet without hunger. After following it, you feel stimulated and strengthened rather than weakened, as you do after the usual dieting. What you get to eat—or, rather, drink—is real nourishment of the richest, most sustaining kind.

To Be Healthy

We live in a scientific age, an age that stresses the value of insurance, that teaches prevention as the better part of wisdom. This one-day-health holiday,* that keeps the body clean by eliminating accumulations of poison and waste and that builds it up with the most concentrated and wholesome forms of nourishment, is the best health insurance you could have.

Liberating the Minerals

Here is another reason for the Health Cocktail:

Much of the nourishment in vegetables is locked in the minute cells of the plant. In this busy age few people take time or trouble to masticate their food sufficiently to get all the nourishment from it. The Health Cocktail contains the concentrated nourishment freed from the plant cells which the lazy individual does not bother to get out.

*"HEALTH DAY"—Bengamin Gayelord Hauser—Tempo Books, Inc., 580 Fifth Avenue, New York.

It was Goethe who called the blood stream "that very special fluid." The juice of the plant is to the plant what the blood stream is to the body, so that when we drink vegetable juices we really drink the life blood of the plant. We get all its life and vitality in this "very special fluid."

Sensitive Stomachs

Health Cocktails are a gift from heaven for those who through years of wrong living have weakened their stomachs.

Plaintively these people say: "I know I need the minerals and the vitamins of fresh fruits and vegetables. But how can I get them when their bulk and roughage are so irritating to me?"

These sufferers have always appealed to my sympathy. Through their own indiscretions, usually, they have cut themselves off from the greatest source of health and physical well-being—fresh fruits and vegetables.

It was their common complaint more than anything else that was responsible for the starting of the Health Cocktail therapy in Carlsbad, the famous spa where thousands of people from all parts of the world crowd each year to seek relief from stomach and intestinal troubles.

Persons with stomach or duodenal ulcers are caught in a vicious circle. They are in desperate need of the minerals and vitamins found in fruits and vegetables. But they must forego this kind of food, because the ulcerated condition of the digestive membranes is easily irritated by the scratchy, rough bulk fibre in which fruit and vegetable juices are held. Therefore the so-called "bland" diets are prescribed for them, made up largely of non-irritating mushes and breadstuffs. To be sure, these diets do not cause irritation to the digestive membranes. But patients held strictly to bland, non-irritating diets never find real health, because the food they are allowed to eat fails to give them the life-bringing minerals.

Health Cocktails give to these sufferers the minerals and chemicals which they so greatly need, in a form that builds up the blood without causing irritation to their impaired digestive systems.

With the appearance of raw-juice therapy, physicians all over the country were eager to try it in cases of ulceration. Results were most satisfactory. Health Cocktails are absolute specifics in intestinal ills.

For here are the precious vitamin and mineral values of all the fruits and vegetables—free from irritating fiber, wholly digestible, soft and soothing, providing nourishment that even an extensively ulcerated case can pick up and use. When the blood stream is replenished once more with vitamins, minerals, healing elements and new life, the patient gains enough strength to heal the indolent ulcer.

For Skinnies

The food you eat must be broken down into simpler chemical forms before it can be transferred to the body cells. Most people who fail to assimilate their food fail to digest it properly. Much of it passes away from them before its value has been extracted. Excessive thinness results.

In malassimilation, whether in adult or

baby, the feeding of fresh vegetable juices brings quick improvement. For these juices are almost automatically assimilated, because of their simple chemical forms.

Thus men and women who have been underweight for years quickly gain needed pounds. Those who have never been able to gather strength to overcome some chronic ailment feel new life surging in them after they learn to drink Health Cocktails.

For the Overweight

Raw juice therapy is a wonderful help for those who wish to reduce. Not only because it cuts down actual food intake, but because it overcomes hidden hunger. I have found that the insatiable food craving that some people have is an unsatisfied hunger for minerals and vitamins. Many concentrated foods have been stripped of their essential elements in processing and refining. When people eat largely of these concentrated foods and neglect the natural foods, the mineral foods, they are starved, even though they may be overweight. The body cells want calcium or iron or vitamin C. Their message to the stomach, brain and intestines is for food—food—food. So the victim eats and eats, but never satisfies the hunger that calls within him. He is starved for minerals.

For convenience this starvation is called hidden hunger. Because we cannot tell exactly which mineral or vitamin is needed we have devised the hidden hunger cocktail. One white vegetable such as parsnips, one yellow—carrots; one green such as spinach and one red—beets; the juice of these four vegetables, representing all the minerals and elements the body requires, is mixed in equal proportions, and we are enabled to drink a hearty toast to the appeasement of the ogre that won't be satisfied—hidden hunger.

Tooth Problems

Nature provided us with teeth for a very definite purpose—to grind and crush foods so that the digestive juices could get into them and do their work. Advancing years, unnecessary tooth pulling and the soft foods of civilization which need little chewing have given many of us a quite inadequate dental equipment. Therefore many people show symptoms of indigestion, distress, gas formation, simply because the food has not been properly masticated and mixed with the digestive juices. For those who have lost their teeth or who have makeshift repairs in their mouths, Health Cocktails are a boon. Here at last is a food they can digest and make use of.

Grandmothers and Grandfathers

Just as the aged should be spared from inclement weather, from hard work, from too much activity, so their digestive systems should be spared the necessity of coping with the digestive problems that the younger stomach is expected to solve.

We feed our babies carefully, methodically. We weigh their food, we modify it, we take special pains in feeding them. We might well give this same courtesy and care to our elders, who have made our lives possible. Were we to prepare grandmother's and grandfather's food with the same care we give to little Johnny's, we might add precious years to their lives.

Health Cocktails provide food in such forms that the delicate aging digestive organs can easily extract nourishment from it; and they tempt the indifferent appetite of old age. Added food value means added years for the aged.

For the Children

There is no denying that most youngsters do not like vegetables. Sometimes the vegetables have no taste, are not properly cooked. In that case you cannot blame the youngsters. Sometimes boys and girls have such an abnormal craving for starches and sweets that their normal taste for salads and vegetables is spoiled.

Raw juice therapy comes to the rescue of the mother confronted with these vegetable dislikes on the part of the child. You can now extract any of the fresh vegetable juices —the richest source of minerals—and for taste you can mix them with the youngster's favorite fresh fruit juice. Most of them like orange juice, grapefruit juice, apple juice, unsweetened pineapple juice and grape juice. These are splendid "mixers" for the vegetable juices. So far I have not found one youngster who did not like the cocktail made with spinach, parsley and orange juice.

Fundamentally these fruit juices are about the same. So mix the vegetable juices with any of the above fruit juices in equal parts.

Greet your boys and girls with one of these vital cocktails when they come home from school. Give your undernourished youngsters two or three glassfuls of this vital juice and almost instantly they will respond with increased strength and vitality.

Psychological Appeal

And now we come to the last—and in some ways the most important—reason for the Health Cocktail.

That is its appeal to the palate, to the eye —all the things that make it psychologically so much more interesting than the vegetables from which it is derived.

It is the thing that makes little Johnny, for instance, smack his lips after a glass of Iron Cocktail when he turns away with real loathing from a mess of boiled spinach prescribed by the doctor because he is anemic. It is the thing that makes grown-ups, as well as children, ask for more.

When it comes to the eye appeal, you can do all sorts of things to produce attractive colors in your Health Cocktails. A little spinach juice gives a pleasing green color; a little beet juice makes an attractive red. And various flavors may be just as easily achieved. Lemon juice, a bit of tomato juice, a little finely chopped watercress, will give you individual taste nuances. In preparing Health Cocktails the housewife has a real opportunity to exercise any artistry and originality she may possess—talents that are stunted by a blind following of the cook book or strict conformity to family food traditions.

It is easy, in speaking of Health Cocktails,

to become almost too enthusiastic about them. For it must be remembered that fruit and vegetable juices cannot take the place of salads and cooked vegetables. The bulk and roughage of fruits and vegetables are very important for the average person; they keep the muscles of the intestines strong and in good working condition.

But Health Cocktails become our *natural medicines* and give us the vital elements in concentrated form when for some reason our digestions are not fitted to handle bulk and roughage. They are also valuable in counteracting the effects of the mass of highly refined foods and complicated mixtures with which we load our digestive systems.

Their uses may vary in extent. The sufferer from stomach ulcers, for example, must depend on them entirely for minerals, chemicals and vitamins. The nervous, dyspeptic housewife who is constantly tired and who looks fagged and worn, can use them advantageously in a one-day health holiday. All of us who are in normal health can vary our menus and add much to the joy of eating by partaking of a sparkling, colorful and delicious Health Cocktail before or between meals.

There is really no limit to what you can do with them. The next time you make cream soup, I suggest that you make it in this way: Heat the milk as usual and after you have turned off the flame add a cup of fresh spinach juice—raw spinach, of course, to be used in its making. This produces a beautiful pastel green color. Add a bit of Meatless Bouillon and, if you like, a bit of whipped cream on top.

All cream soups can be made in this way. Besides cream of spinach soup you may try cream of beet soup or cream of carrot soup. And here is a new idea—cream of pea-pod soup. All of them can be made in a jiffy.

In all cooking remember not to add salt *while* the food is on the fire. It toughens the food and takes twice as much time to cook. Add salt only *after* the flame has been turned off. This brings out the natural flavor of the food; and then you can add a bit of vegetable salt (Nu-Vege-Sal) which gives additional flavour and savour.

And now I pass on to you my best formulas to start you along the Trail of the Cocktail Shaker. Once you have gone a little way, you will find exciting byways of your own to follow.

The Selection of Foods

Choose solid, heavy fruits and vegetables. The heavier they are for their size, the more juice they contain.

Select young, tender, fresh vegetables, with leaves still green and crisp. The deep orange-colored California carrots make the best juice.

Smooth, small-leafed spinach is the tenderest and best flavored.

Heavy, crisp, green-leafed celery makes the richest juice.

Use the leaves and roots of vegetables. They are rich in minerals. They may be made into separate drinks or mixed. Carrot tops are very rich in minerals, making a strong medicine, to be used sparingly.

Watercress, rich in sulphur, should also be used in small portions.

Remember, in choosing vegetables for your Health Cocktails, that their juices are all used raw. Cooking spoils their tonic value. Hence the vegetables must all be fresh and in good condition.

Preparation of Vegetables

Vegetables are quickly and safely cleaned by this simple method:

Put a handful of ordinary salt in a dish-pan of cold water and let the vegetables stand, uncut, in it for twenty minutes. Remove any insects. The few drops of lemon juice you always have in your fruit cup will destroy any germs. Rinse, cut out any spoiled portions. Use the whole vegetable. Leaves, skin and roots contain valuable minerals.

Be sure not to cut the vegetables before cleaning, because salt water would leech out the mineral elements in them.

After washing, cut the vegetables with long, tough strings, such as celery, beet stems, rhubarb and peapods, into one and one-half inch pieces.

Either quarter or cut into lengthwise sections to fit behind the teeth of the grinding shaft all root or solid fruits or vegetables, such as beets, carrots, cucumbers, apples, pineapples, etc.

Fine fiber foods, such as carrots, onions, apples, radishes, and cucumbers, may be put through the extractor twice.

For those of you with intestinal ills or in weakened condition an extra cleansing precaution is worth while. For as long as our farmers do not know how to chemicalize their soil they will have difficulties with all kinds of pests. Unfortunately they now use various kinds of sprays which can be harmful to those in a weakened condition. So if you are put on a vegetable diet you might take advantage of the following formula I use:

Removing Poison Sprays

Buy at your druggist's one ounce of chemically pure hydrochloric acid. Mix this thoroughly with three quarts of water. This is approximately a one per cent solution. The spray-remover is kept in an earthenware crock. Vegetables used are first washed in the ordinary manner, then placed for five minutes in the spray-remover, removed and rinsed in water again. The spray-remover solution can be used by the average family of five for about a week. Should a little of the hydrochloric acid remain on the vegetables it will do no harm. In this weak solution it is practically the same as is normally present in the stomach.

RULES FOR MAKING PERFECT JUICES

1. There are several machines on the market for extracting juices from vegetables. I recommend the use of the Health-Mine Juice Extractor which was designed especially for me. This machine is by far the easiest and simplest to use. The Health-Mine Juice Extractor may be obtained at Health Food Stores or hardware stores or direct from the manufacturers, Modern Health Products Supply Co., 1428 N. Twenty Fourth St., Milwaukee, Wis.
2. Vegetables must be carefully cleaned for making juices. Sick people should wash their vegetables in a weak hydrochloric acid solution, as given on page 25.
3. Vegetables such as celery and rhubarb should be cut in two-inch pieces to prevent stringing.
4. When leaves such as spinach, lettuce or dandelion are used, it is wise to mix in some of the stems and if possible some of the roots.
5. All vegetable juices perish quickly and lose their color at once. To prevent this have a

bit of lemon or grapefruit juice in the cup into which juice flows. Carrots taste better with orange juice.

6. Raw vegetable juices are splendid medicines and can be taken indefinitely. However, best results are obtained by the regular use of from one and a half cups to not more than three cups a day. Vegetable juices are best fresh but will keep in a cool place for twenty-four hours.

RECIPES

AND

INSTRUCTIONS

To Be Healthy

CELERY COCKTAIL

INGREDIENTS

Fresh, Crisp Celery

Lemon Juice

METHOD

Wash celery. Cut stalks into two-inch pieces and put through the Health-Mine. Have the juice of half a lemon in the cup into which the celery juice flows. This adds tempting flavor and preserves the clear, fresh color of this sparkling cocktail.

(It is best not to use too many of the celery leaves, as they make the juice too bitter.)

One and a half cups of this juice is a good daily ration for one person. This cup and a half is divided into three cocktails—preferably to be taken between meals and before retiring.

The Celery Cocktail should be made fresh every day.

This Celery Cocktail is a specific against:

Indigestion

Sour Stomach

All forms of Rheumatism

IRON COCKTAIL

INGREDIENTS

Crisp, Dark Green Spinach

Fresh Parsley

Orange Juice for Flavor

METHOD

Put well washed spinach and parsley through the Health-Mine. Two large handfuls of spinach, a small handful of parsley, is the best proportion.

This juice, rich in iron and copper, makes a potent body-building tonic but is not pleasant to the taste. For this reason it is mixed with orange juice—about half and half.

Three cups a day of this spinach, parsley and orange juice makes a splendid cocktail and is easily taken by those who "hate spinach."

This Iron Cocktail is a specific in all forms of anemia and is an all-round building tonic.

To Be Healthy

CARROT COCKTAIL

INGREDIENTS

Golden Carrots

Orange Juice

METHOD

Scrub carrots until their skin glows and sparkles. Cut into vertical strips about one half inch wide and put through the Health-Mine.

(If you prefer you may shred the carrots on a medium sized shredder and then put them through the Health-Mine.)

This juice deteriorates very easily and loses its golden color. For this reason you must have some orange juice in the cup into which the juice flows.

Since carrots are quite dry and do not give much juice you may put them twice through the Health-Mine.

Mix the carrot juice with the orange juice in equal proportions.

This Carrot Cocktail, if faithfully imbibed, is warranted to produce that schoolgirl complexion.

CABBAGE COCKTAIL

INGREDIENTS

Fresh Young Cabbage (The younger the cabbage, the better the juice!)

Lemon Juice

Grapefruit Juice for Palatability

METHOD

Cut fresh cabbage into slices and put through the Health-Mine.

To keep the cocktail crystal clear put a bit of lemon juice in the cup into which the cabbage juice flows.

In this form it is a vital reducing drink. To make it more palatable, combine two-thirds cabbage juice and one-third grapefruit juice.

Three cups of this cocktail is all that is needed in one day. It can be taken before meals as an appetizer or between meals.

This Cabbage Cocktail contains: Chlorine, Iron and Magnesium.

It is splendid for reducing the waistline and for correcting faulty elimination.

RED CABBAGE COCKTAIL

INGREDIENTS

Fresh Red Cabbage

Unsweetened Pineapple Juice

METHOD

Cut the red cabbage, nicely cleaned, into slices and put through the Health-Mine. The juice flows easily and the color is an attractive vermilion. To preserve this color and to make a most appetizing combination, add unsweetened pineapple juice, either fresh or canned.

Juice from the red cabbage, like that from the white, is a good reducing drink. But you must not spoil the combination by using more pineapple juice than cabbage juice. Two-thirds of red cabbage juice and one-third of pineapple juice is a most delicious combination.

This Red Cabbage Cocktail is a specific reducing cocktail. It may be served as an appetizer before meals or at any time between meals.

CUCUMBER COCKTAIL

INGREDIENTS

Young Cucumbers

Grapefruit Juice

METHOD

Cut unpeeled cucumbers into slices and put them through the Health-Mine. Since cucumbers are about 70% "live water" you will get a lot of juice.

Grapefruit juice added to the cucumber juice sets the delicate color and improves the flavor. Equal amounts make the finest taste.

Because cucumbers are a natural diuretic kidney flush, not more than one and one-half cups should be taken daily.

Cucumber juice deteriorates very quickly so it should immediately be put into the refrigerator.

This Cucumber Cocktail is a specific for the system, especially for the kidneys. Puffs under the eyes have been known to disappear after the use of this natural medicine.

BEET COCKTAIL

INGREDIENTS

Young Tender Beet Roots

A Few Young Leaves

Pineapple Juice

METHOD

Cut up the beets and leaves and put them through the Health-Mine. A beautiful ruby-tinted "vegetable wine" will flow into your cup.

To retain the color and to make the cocktail more tasty, you may add fresh or canned pineapple juice (unsweetened). Half and half makes the right combination.

This cocktail is highly alkaline. It has high appetite appeal, because of its flavor and because of its wine-like hue. It makes a splendid change among the health cocktails.

This Beet Cocktail is a specific for driving out acids and is a general building tonic.

RADISH COCKTAIL

INGREDIENTS

Radishes—White, Red, or (still better) the Large black Variety

Lemon Juice

METHOD

Cut the radishes into small pieces and put through the Health-Mine. The younger they are the better they are, for the more juice they will yield. So choose them young and fresh.

The color of the cocktail depends on the variety of radish you use. The small red ones make a very attractive cocktail. Be sure to have some lemon juice in the cup into which the radish juice flows.

This wholesome juice is rich in sulphur and is a rather strong medicine. Therefore not more than one cupful a day two or three times a week should be taken.

To tickle the palate with radish juice mix it with grapefruit juice—half and half.

This Radish Cocktail, because of its sulphur, is a potent tonic and a powerful cleanser for the gall bladder.

WATERCRESS COCKTAIL

INGREDIENTS

Crisp Watercress

Fresh Parsley or Spinach

Orange Juice

METHOD

Watercress is rich in mustard oil, so it is better to mix it with some other milder green, such as parsley or spinach.

Put equal parts of the watercress and either parsley or spinach through the Health-Mine. There will be plenty of dark green juice, rich in minerals and vitamins.

To give it an appealing taste add some orange juice. Equal amounts are best.

This combination is a powerful cleanser and must be taken in small amounts. Two cocktails a day of one-half cup each are all that should be taken.

This Watercress Cocktail is a specific for blood purification and because of its high alkaline content it helps drive out rheumatic poisons.

COCKTAIL MIXTE

INGREDIENTS

Cabbage, Crisp and Fresh

Celery, Ditto

Green Pepper, Sound and Firm

Lemon or Grapefruit Juice

METHOD

Put equal parts of cabbage and celery, with a bit of green pepper for flavor, through the Health-Mine.

This makes a very well balanced mixture which is rich in iron, sodium and sulphur.

But for a drink that is utterly delicious, as well as wholesome, add a bit of lemon or grapefruit juice.

This Cocktail can be taken three times a day (one-half cup each time), preferably between meals.

SPRING COCKTAIL

INGREDIENTS

Tender Rhubarb

Fresh Strawberries

A Little Honey

METHOD

The fresh, tender stalks of rhubarb contain Nature's natural laxative elements. Fresh strawberries are potent in cleansing and beautifying elements.

Equal parts of tender rhubarb and fresh strawberries put through the Health-Mine make a rose-colored juice as beautiful as it is wholesome.

To prevent stringing, cut rhubarb stalks in two-inch pieces.

A little honey to sweeten the cocktail makes this juice even more delicious.

Two cupfuls a day is enough.

This Cocktail, especially in the springtime, is a powerful drink to purify the system and clean up a muddy complexion.

DE-TOXICANT COCKTAIL

INGREDIENTS

Garlic, About Three Cloves*

Parsley, a Large Handful

Green Pepper, Just a Bit

METHOD

Garlic is Nature's most powerful germicidal herb. Unfortunately its odor is so strong that most people never use it. This Health Cocktail offers a new and pleasant way of taking garlic without advertising the fact to the world.

Put all the ingredients through the Health-Mine. The parsley juice is rich in copper and iron and helps to destroy the strong odor of garlic.

The organic sulphur in garlic is a powerful cleanser for the entire intestinal tract.

This De-Toxicant Cocktail can be taken two or three times a week, preferably before retiring. It is especially good for those suffering from excessive gas.

*If fresh garlic is unobtainable add one-quarter teaspoonful of Santay Garlic Powder to the Parsley Juice.

ENDOCRINE COCKTAIL

INGREDIENTS

Egg Yolks, One Tablespoonful

Yellow Olive Oil, One Quarter Teaspoonful

Sea Greens, One Quarter Teaspoonful

Juice of Two Oranges

METHOD

Mix the egg yolks, olive oil, Sea Greens and Orange Juice and beat until foamy.

A bit of orange peel, shredded very fine, should top this cocktail.

The nerve and glandular oils with the Sea Greens supply the proper nourishment for the glands.

Orange peel, finely shredded, is a splendid means of providing the sunshine vitamin D.

Not more than one of these cocktails should be taken every day.

DANDELION COCKTAIL

INGREDIENTS

Dandelion Leaves

Parsley or Green Onions

Lemon or Grapefruit Juice

METHOD

Dandelions are rich in potassium, iron and other alkaline elements, especially if you get the wild variety. Since these greens are very bitter it is best to mix them with parsley or green onions.

Use equal amounts. Put them through the Health-Mine to make a rich dark green juice.

Add grapefruit juice or lemon juice to taste, for the sake of palatability.

Not more than two cupfuls a day of this potent juice should be taken.

This Dandelion Cocktail is beneficial to those who are sluggish and tired.

ANTI-COLD COCKTAILS

1. Wash a juicy grapefruit and cut into slices. Put peeling, seeds and all through the Health-Mine.

This makes a strong, rather bitter juice which has specific properties for breaking up colds.

For flavor, add some honey.

Drink a glassful of this juice at least three times a day, preferably in the morning, at noon and before retiring.

2. Cut up two large, juicy oranges, peeling and all, and put through the Health-Mine.

This orange juice is rich in Vitamin C and the peeling is saturated with the sunshine Vitamin D, a powerful factor in breaking up colds.

For best results this cocktail should be taken about every two hours.

PARTY COCKTAIL

INGREDIENTS

Grapefruit Juice

Italian Celery (Also Called Fenuchi or Anise)

METHOD

You may use fresh or canned grapefruit juice. To one cupful add one tablespoonful of the fresh juice extracted from the Italian celery.

This makes a delicious and interesting drink that will make your guests think you are serving a French absinthe.

Unsweetened pineapple juice may be used in place of the grapefruit juice. This combination is piquant and tempting.

If you must put a "stick" in this cocktail, let your conscience be your guide.

This Party Cocktail is a specific against gloom and depression.

GLORIFIED TOMATO COCKTAILS

Tomato juice has so many good properties by itself that it has become, within a few years, America's most popular vegetable drink.

A good brand of canned tomato juice is almost as good as the fresh juice. It has the big advantage of being inexpensive at all seasons and of being ever ready to use.

You can serve tomato juice in many tempting ways. Here is a new one: Add celery juice—about equal proportions of the two give the best drink. This makes a remarkable drink with lots of tang. Add a dash of Hungarian spice* and your cocktail will be the hit of the party.

THE LAZY ANN COCKTAIL

This cocktail can be made in a jiffy. Fresh cabbage juice is added to tomato juice. Two-thirds tomato juice to one-third cabbage juice gives a tempting result. And here is the Lazy Ann way: Mix two-thirds tomato juice and one-third sauerkraut juice. This is a refreshing cocktail, mixed in a second, and it helps to reduce bulging waistlines.

*Nu-Spice (Hungarian style), Nu-Vege-Sal, Santay Garlic Powder, Meatless Bouillon and other important accessory foods may be obtained at your health food store or direct from the manufacturers, Modern Health Products, Inc., 1428 North 24th Street, Milwaukee, Wisconsin.

GLORIFIED POTASSIUM BROTH

INGREDIENTS

Celery, One Bunch

Carrots, One Bunch

Spinach, a Handful

Parsley, a Pinch

Vegetable Salt, One Teaspoonful or Meatless Bouillon, One Tablespoonful

METHOD

Everyone knows and likes my Potassium Broth. Here is a way of adding more flavour and savour:

Cut the vegetables fine or put them through an ordinary chopper. When finely shredded or cut there should be about three cups of celery, three of carrots and one of spinach. Our pinch of parsley should yield about a quarter cup. Add two quarts of water and cook from twenty to thirty minutes—not more. After the flame has been turned out add one level teaspoonful of vegetable salt (Nu-Vege-Sal) or, if you like a meat-like flavor, add a tablespoonful of Meatless Bouillon. To further vitalize and glorify this alkaline broth, you may add (after the flame has been turned off) one cup of your favorite vegetable juice, such as fresh or canned tomato juice, celery juice, or pea-pod juice. This broth may be served hot or it may be chilled and served as an appetizer.

YOUR OWN RECIPES

YOUR OWN RECIPES

YOUR OWN RECIPES

YOUR OWN RECIPES

YOUR OWN RECIPES

YOUR OWN RECIPES

YOUR OWN RECIPES

YOUR OWN RECIPES

FOOD SCIENCE AND HEALTH

PRESENTS in simple language the fascinating facts about practical food science as it may be used in your daily life for the promotion of better health and greater efficiency. This volume contains in detailed form the famous Hauser Eliminative Feeding System. This is not a "diet" but a seven day feeding system during which time the entire system is flushed and re-chemicalized by eating an abundance of the best foods on earth. The Eliminative Feeding System completely antiquates the many old fashioned freak diets and dangerous fasts and introduces a new era of feeding based on sound scientific facts, proven practical and enthusiastically endorsed by thousands of users throughout the world. $2.00.

TEMPO BOOKS, INC., · 580 FIFTH AVE., NEW YORK, N. Y.

BOOKS BY BENGAMIN GAYELORD HAUSER

HARMONIZED FOOD SELECTION

THE subject of food chemistry is given very little thought by the average individual and yet the foods we eat and the combinations in which we eat them have everything in the world to do with our daily health and well being. This volume brings to you vital knowledge which you may use to re-build your body and supply to your muscles, bones, nervous and glandular system, those foods which they require for more efficient functioning. Once you have read this book and are familiar with the principles presented therein, you will be able to balance your own meals and eat for health in a sane and delightful manner without the fear of becoming a "diet crank." $2.00.

TEMPO BOOKS, INC., · 580 FIFTH AVE., NEW YORK, N. Y.

NEW HEALTH COOKERY

SIMPLY to label a recipe healthful was not enough for Bengamin Gayelord Hauser and his staff of nutritionists. They insisted that each recipe pass a double test —it must be delicious to taste as well as healthful. The result is an amazing collection of the most delightful things to eat—and all of them made without such harmful ingredients as denatured flours and sugar, vinegar and animal fats. None of the joy of eating is lost in these splendid recipes. New ways of preparing vegetables so they retain all their healthful qualities and garden-fresh color. New ideas for salads, a whole section devoted to meat substitutes and even meats themselves, soups and desserts—all are found in this new health cookery. $2.00.

Tempo Books, Inc., · 580 Fifth Ave., New York, N. Y.

Books By Bengamin Gayelord Hauser

CHILD FEEDING

Written for Mothers

THE modern mother starts feeding her child at the time of conception. In guarding her own health and diet during pregnancy she can give her baby a strong healthy body. In this book, Bengamin Gayelord Hauser has released a wealth of knowledge on the subject of Child Feeding through the various stages of infancy, childhood and adolescence. If his methods are followed, a child has a far greater chance of growing into splendid manhood or womanhood. $2.50.

TEMPO BOOKS, INC., · 580 FIFTH AVE., NEW YORK, N. Y.

Printed in U. S. A.

9 781430 477532

CPSIA information can be obtained
at www.ICGtesting.com
Printed in the USA
LVHW101236300623
751256LV00002B/6

9 781161 628487